Growing Up in my AMISH WORLD

Eirene Eicher

Growing Up Amish, Second Edition

Copyright © 2021 Eirene Eicher, All rights reserved
Contact: www.eireneeicher.com | EicherIrene7@gmail.com

Copyright protects the voice of the author, encourages diversity of thought, creates space for uninhibited creativity, and adds value to the human experience. Thank you for buying this book and thereby promoting free speech. No portion of this book may be reproduced mechanically, electronically, or by any other means, including photocopy, without permission of the publisher or author except in the case of brief quotations embodied in critical articles and reviews. It is illegal to copy this book, post it to a website, or distribute by any other means without permission from the publisher or author.

The purpose of this book is to educate and entertain as a work of creative nonfiction. The author and/or publisher shall have neither liability nor responsibility to anyone with respect to any loss or damage caused, or alleged to be caused, directly or indirectly by the information contained in this book. Events are portrayed to the best of the author's memory. The story, experiences and words are the author's alone.

Photographs from the author's collection

Cover Design and Formatting: Meg Delagrange

PRINTED IN THE UNITED STATES OF AMERICA

Contents

1. MEET MY SIBLINGS	7
2. IN THE HOUSE	25
3. ON THE FARM	37
4. AT SCHOOL	45
5. TRIPS TO OHIO	53
6. MY TEENAGE YEARS	63

*I dedicate this book to my Mom and Dad.
I couldn't have asked for better parents.
I treasure my childhood because of you.*

My baby sister and me.

I.

Meet My Siblings

I have fun memories of growing up with my siblings, sixteen brothers and sisters in all, fourteen who are still living. There are particular traits about each of them that I hold dear to my heart. I'll always cherish the close bond we shared and the fun memories we made while we were chasing cows, teasing each other, and falling asleep under the stars beside the river with Uncle Johnny. Before I tell you about some of our adventures, let me introduce you to my siblings.

Benjamin

FIRSTBORN

• •

Benjamin is the brother that I never met, who found his heavenly wings at just three weeks old. Mom was devastated at the loss of her most beautiful, dark-haired angel, who developed an infection in the blood and passed on into heaven as a newborn baby.

MEET MY SIBLINGS

Samuel

A TWIN TO MANUEL

PERSONALITY: OUTGOING & SARCASTIC

••••••••••••••••••••••••••••

No one could tell my twin brothers apart, but I could. Samuel had a twinkle in his eye and an insatiable taste for adventure. It was his idea to switch places with his brother at school one day, and their teacher never knew the difference.

Manuel

A TWIN TO SAMUEL

PERSONALITY:
COMPASSIONATE & SOFT-HEARTED

• •

Manuel may have been the softie, but he wasn't ever left out of any adventure. He was right beside Samuel during every barrel race. They also raced two ponies that looked alike, racing up and down the road in their little carts, hitched to the ponies. It was Manuel who constantly checked on me to make sure that I was okay.

MEET MY SIBLINGS

Eirene

FOURTH BORN

PERSONALITY: PRETTY TOMGIRL

••••••••••••••••••••••••••••

Always up for an adventure with my older twin brothers, I jumped into life and rode her for all she could give me. My long, dark, wavy hair was always parted in the center and pulled back into a bun under my cap. I borrowed my brothers' pants to clean out the pig pens, poop coming up to my ankles, working alongside my brothers to muck out the barn. My philosophy was — if my brothers could do it, so could I!

Christina

FIFTH BORN

**PERSONALITY:
SHY**

• •

The second-born girl in the family, Christina, followed me around everywhere I went. She and I sang together in beautiful harmony and worked on the household chores together. It was always fun to tease Christina because it was easy to get her agitated and upset. I'd get her agitated while we were doing dishes, and then Christina would chase me around the yard, crying, while I laughed. It wasn't funny then, but we do laugh about it now.

Dena

SIXTH BORN

PERSONALITY: STRONG-WILLED

• •

Dena was more stubborn than all fourteen kids put together. Dena was also brilliant. One of the men that dad worked with used to say, "Irene's got the looks, Dena's got the brains." She would have been a sharp and successful businesswoman, but she's busy raising a large family and married to an Amish bishop.

Mary

SEVENTH BORN

PERSONALITY:
EASY GOING & FUN LOVING

• •

Everyone loves Mary. She's very fun-loving and loves to tease. As a girl, she'd pop up into any space with a bright smile or a giggle. She's the only sister who also left the Amish.

Noah

EIGHTH BORN

PERSONALITY:
VERY SWEET & COMPASSIONATE

••••••••••••••••••••••••••••

Noah is one of the most compassionate out of all nine brothers. He has a gift for showing up for others. Later in life, when I was in the hospital because of a heart condition, my brother Noah visited me. He loves sharing a meal with family or celebrating a birthday.

Margaret

NINTH BORN

PERSONALITY:
SHY, YET FRIENDLY

• •

Margaret is the loyal one in the family. She considers her family as still being her family, even when we disagree with each other, and she's always willing to help wherever and whenever any of us need her. Family values are essential to her. Today she is married to an Amish preacher.

Solomon

TENTH BORN

PERSONALITY:
INTELLIGENT & HARDWORKING

••••••••••••••••••••••••••••

Everything Solomon touches turns to gold. He's also very daring — there's nothing that would scare him. When he cut his thumb badly while working on the job and it needed stitches, he just grabbed his handkerchief to wrap around it and kept on working. There's no stopping Solomon. He always gets the job done, no matter what!

Mervin

ELEVENTH BORN

PERSONALITY:
FRIENDLY & FUN-LOVING

••••••••••••••••••••••••••••••

Mervin is hardworking, just like his older brother, but not as outgoing as Solomon. He was mischievous as a boy, and he still loves to have fun. Today he's a good uncle who keeps in touch with his nieces and nephews.

Elmer

TWELFTH BORN

PERSONALITY:
DEEP & THOUGHTFUL

••••••••••••••••••••••••••••

Elmer is the shyest out of all of us. He simply won't say much. As a boy, he was bashful and a rule follower, the one who wouldn't ever get into trouble. He had a rock-solid commitment to the Amish Ordnung, and he grew up to become an Amish preacher.

Paul

THIRTEENTH BORN

PERSONALITY:
FRIENDLY & FUN-LOVING

• •

Paul was a very sweet kid. I was fourteen when he was born, and I was there with Mom in the room when he came into this world. Paul was like my own baby. I took care of him from birth and kept him close to me until I got married. Paul is as good as they come, wholesome and handsome.

Vernon

FOURTEENTH BORN

PERSONALITY: ADVENTUROUS

• •

Vernon was born after I got married, but he's grown up into the type of person that will be a friend for life. He's a peacemaker and morally conscious. Like the rest of his brothers, he's a hard worker with an ambitious drive to succeed, but there's not a selfish bone in his body. He is very generous and takes good care of our Mom.

Ernest

FIFTEENTH BORN

....

Ernest only lived six months before passing away from a heart defect. We all mourned the loss of this precious baby and the life we never got to have with him.

MEET MY SIBLINGS

Michael

SIXTEENTH BORN

PERSONALITY:
QUIET REBEL

••••••••••••••••••••••••••••

I didn't get to witness Michael's growing up years because he was also born after I left home, and he was the youngest. He's younger than my oldest son! Michael is probably the quietest person you'll ever meet, but that doesn't mean he likes to follow the rules. He listened to music that he wasn't supposed to listen to and pushed the boundaries, but quietly. He's a quiet rebel. Michael always liked to explore other options, so it's no surprise that he isn't Amish today. He moves from one state to the next, like a quiet wanderer.

Me, having a conversation inside our house.

2.

In The House

I will forever admire my mother's ability to whip up a delicious meal at a moment's notice. She was a talented cook. My four sisters and I gleaned that trait from her. She taught us how to be good cooks and how to keep lovely, clean homes, and how to sew, plant gardens, and can food. She taught us so much, and she did it in love. Very seldom do I remember her getting impatient with any of her sixteen children. No matter how many children she had, she was always excited about having another one on the way.

Since the twins were thirteen months older than me, they got to go to school before me. I was the oldest girl, so I shouldered most of the workload in the house, helping my Mom. It seemed there was always a lot of work with our fast-growing family. I learned how to do household chores at a very young age.

After the twins got on the bus, my sisters and I had to do the dishes. I was seven, and Christina was five. As you might imagine, I was not fond of the task. I was the oldest, so it was my job to wash while Christina dried the dishes. I stood on a stool to reach the sink pans, but my arms were so short that the sudsy dishwater always ran down my arms, making my dress wet.

There were days when we lollygagged around, doing dishes all day long. We would still be doing dishes when the boys got off the bus in the afternoon. Before lunch dishes were done, it was time to cook dinner and do the dishes all over again.

I teased Christina mercilessly because it was so much fun to tease her. I knew just what to say to push her buttons, and then she'd chase me all over the house and out the door, calling out to Mom. Mom was too busy to pay attention to our little squabbles as she worked away at the sewing machine or any one of a number of things a busy mother had to do. I laughed while Christina cried. I'm sure I owe her a huge apology. She knew I loved her and for the most part, we got along great. As we got older, we became the best of friends.

Endless mountains of laundry felt like a never-ending job each week since we had to carry all the water in buckets from the water pump to the washbasin to wash the clothes. As I got older, more of the responsibility for the laundry fell on my shoulders. It was always a relief when Mom would decide to hire someone to drive us with baskets and baskets of clothes to the laundromat in town. That was so much easier than handwashing and rinsing the clothes and hanging them out on the clothesline to dry. This also cut down on ironing since we would hang the clothes on hangers as we took them out of the dryers. While we were at the laundromat, I loved watching people. That was my favorite part.

It seemed like every other year, another baby was born to our family. As I got older, my Mom would deliver the baby at home. I got to clean up my new baby siblings and dress them in the new, homemade baby gowns. My Mom used to say, "I wish I had two Irenes," which made me feel needed and appreciated.

The kitchen was extra warm in the summertime because we used the kerosene cookstove to prepare any cooked meals. In the wintertime, we were all drawn to the crackle of the fire in the woodstove in the family room with its deep, penetrating warmth. That big wood stove had a way of making us feel right at home. I absolutely loved the smell of the burning wood and the crackling sounds as the fire burned in the stove.

IN THE HOUSE

On the weekends, Mom helped us as we poured water into stainless steel boilers, big rectangular-shaped kettles that sat on the big wood stove to heat up water for our baths. The stove was fired up with plenty of wood beforehand. The house that we grew up in still had a bathtub in it from the Englisha that lived in it before us, and dad didn't tear it out, so we poured the hot water in it to take baths. All of us shared the same tub full of water to get clean. Sometimes, we also used galvanized tubs for bathing.

After bathing, we put on our nighties and lit the kerosene lanterns in our rooms. Without hair dryers, I would sit up and read late into the night until my hair dried. I loved reading because it would take me into another world. I could easily read until midnight and even later. My uncle, who was an Amish Bishop, would tell me, "Reading is good for you, it broadens your mind."

I loved reading true stories about our forefathers, the Anabaptists. They were so in love with

Christ that they willingly burned at the stake for their faith. It made me curious about what it would be like to have faith like that.

One of the most influential books I read was about the Anabaptists, not even realizing this was where my roots came from. The book was called 'The Martyrs' Mirror'. It described true accounts of how the Early Church and our ancestors, the Anabaptist, were tortured for their faith and their uncompromising love for God. They willingly gave their lives for Christ.

Our Amish forefathers actually come from the Anabaptist movement. They began in Switzerland within a group of Swiss and Alsatian Anabaptists in 1693, led by a man by the name of Jakob Ammann. Those who followed Ammann became known as Amish. They first came to America in the 1700s and settled near Lancaster, Pennsylvania, where there is a very large Amish community still to this day. Eventually, the Amish migrated west to form new communities, such as the one that I was born into.

I wondered how one man could decide to break away from his church and start a new denomination called by his own name and convince thousands and thousands of people to follow his teachings and place them in the ban if they didn't follow him, where they would be shunned for the rest of their life or as long as they didn't return to his church in repentance. Was this true Christianity or merely a man-made religion? That's where the Amish began their denomination. The day would come when I'd find the answers to these perplexing questions.

There are many different Sects of Amish. Each Sect has its own 'Ordnung or church letter. These are rules set by each church's Bishop and ministers. They believe that if two or three of them agree on this Ordnung, it carries the same weight on earth as if it was done in heaven. Each church district is divided geographically. What is allowed in one church may be considered a sin in another, and so if there's something that is allowed in one district that makes life easier, a person would have to move into that district in order for it to not be a sin for them to have it.

In some of the churches, cigarettes are considered a sin but smoking the pipe was permitted. I vividly remember the sweet aroma from my grandpa's pipe as we sat in the barn where he lazily smoked his pipe. He seemed to enjoy it immensely as one of the joys of his life when he wasn't working in the fields or building something for someone in his shop.

I read about how the Anabaptist martyr's faces would shine from the Glory of God and how they would sing while being burned alive at the stake. I could not fathom that kind of faith. I was very intrigued by their love for Jesus, and how they were willing to die for their faith in Christ. I wondered what it was that I would have had to give up if I were ever questioned about my faith. Would I just not wear my Amish clothes? Is that what defined my faith? What was the Anabaptist faith? I didn't know but, I hungered for the kind of love, peace, and joy they experienced. This was where the hunger for Christ started in my heart. I knew there had to be more to life than what I was being taught. I asked myself these questions and many more.

There are times when I wonder how we did everything that we did without electricity or running water, especially when we would prepare for big events like weddings. It would take us days or weeks to get ready and required the help of many people to prepare the feast for the big day.

The Amish are known for their delicious cooking, so you can imagine that going to an Amish wedding is a treat. The meals usually consist of fried or grilled chicken, buttery mashed potatoes with gravy, dressing, a vegetable, and a couple of different salads or cottage cheese for the sides. Later, a variety of delicious desserts are served to the guests. Oh, they are the tastiest desserts. The Pecan and Sugar Cream pies are two of my favorites.

Then there are the Apple Crumb, Cherry, and Peanut Butter Pies. Just the thought of them makes my mouth water. I also loved the flakey *knee patches* that were placed on each table. These consisted of a very thin crust deep fried with sugar on them. They weren't very nutritious, but they were one of the most delicious wedding treats.

The wedding feast is different from the simple lunch that we served after a church service, but that one is equally as delicious. Church meals consist of a homemade peanut butter mixture spread on bread, with a few sides. I still make homemade peanut butter spread to this day. I usually use crunchy peanut butter, marshmallow cream, and white Karo syrup to make it. Mix it all together for a delicious gooey sandwich. I love this with a slice of Bologna and Colby cheese. At church meals, some people would serve Bologna with the peanut butter sandwiches, but not everyone liked that. They'd also serve pickled beets and sweet bread and butter pickles to complement the sandwiches. It may all sound very strange to you, but it is mouthwateringly delicious.

Even though not all Amish Sects see eye to eye, the one thing they all have in common is camaraderie. If someone needs a helping hand, they drop their differences and help each other. It doesn't matter how big or small the job is, they get together and do the work that needs to be done. They can build a barn in a day. They can butcher multiple hogs in a short time. Many hands make light the work, they say.

The women work just as hard as the men, taking care of the children and feeding the hungry workers. Within an hour, they can cook up a huge meal which sometimes consists of homemade beef and noodles, mashed potatoes, mixed vegetables, salad, and of course, their delicious, freshly baked bread. There's nothing better than that.

These are some of the many things I loved about growing up in my Amish community.

The farm where our cousins lived.

3.

On The Farm

Life on the farm was delightful. Believe it or not, I actually miss the days of working alongside my siblings on the farm. It made the chores seem pleasant by doing them together while chatting or singing and yodeling. Some of those chores consisted of working side by side in the garden, planting seeds, pulling weeds, and such. I enjoyed the outdoor work, mowing the grass with a push-mower and painting the buggies.

We always had something to do, from skipping down the cow path to bringing the cows in for milking time, cleaning out the stinky pig pens, and climbing up to the hayloft to throw down the hay bales. We usually ended up frolicking around in the hay, hanging onto the long thick ropes that hung from the rafters and swinging from one loft to another. Oh the fun I had, all the while wearing my little Amish dress. We girls were not allowed to wear pants, which would have been much more appropriate for all of the activities on the farm, I am sure. I did borrow a pair of my brother's pants to clean out the pig pens in the barn. The poop was so deep it came up to my ankles.

I absolutely adored my older twin brothers and they didn't seem to mind me trailing along behind them. Sometimes they would ask me to choose which one of the two that I liked the best. Of course, I couldn't choose one over the other. I dearly loved them both and absolutely loved all the fun times we had together. I also shared their love of all our animals, especially the horses. We had two ponies that looked like twins and my brothers would go barrel racing on them or hitch them up to race up and down the road.

My twin brothers are only thirteen months older than me and I loved following them all around the farm, even when that meant following them up the ladder to the top of the barn roof. On one such day, my dad and his employees were out in the yard chatting after a long day at work. It was very windy, I was wearing my little Amish dress, and as I climbed up the ladder, the wind whipped my dress up over my head, leaving my little underwear-clad bottom exposed for all to see. I never did hear the end of that from Ervin, one of my dad's employees. What an embarrassment for a conservative little Amish girl! I will never forget that day as long as I live.

Sometimes my brothers and I would walk over to the neighbors, who were also our cousins. They had a much bigger farm than ours and we loved to watch them as they milked the cows and did their chores. It was summertime, and the barns had no air conditioning. Cows would swat at the flies with their tails, hitting anyone sitting next to them right in the face. Sometimes my cousins would sing and yodel as they milked the cows, which made the job a little more pleasant.

It was satisfying to watch as they poured bucket after bucket of the rich milk into the milk strainers, which they set up over five-gallon galvanized cans. They'd set the cans into cement tanks with cold water to keep them at the right temperature until the milkman would come to pick them up. Even the cleanup was fun to watch. They used huge stainless steel strainers and buckets, which had to be washed and sterilized after each use. It looked like a lot of work, but they made it seem fun.

My brothers and I loved to go down to the river, camping with our Uncle Johnny. He is one of my favorite uncles on my Mom's side of the family. Johnny is the youngest of Mom's siblings. I'll never forget his infectious jolly laugh. He never seemed to take life too seriously and always pushed the limits. He could play any instrument he picked up or put his mind to learn. He doesn't seem to mind that playing these instruments is against the church rules.

He would tell us stories as we kids nodded off to sleep in our sleeping bags. I remember the joy of those summer evenings — roasting hot dogs over the crackling bonfire, the smoky smell as we piled more logs on the fire, and the sounds of the night critters in the woods. The sounds of nature, water trickling in the river, and the crickets singing were and are to this day, music to my ears and soothing to my soul.

I loved waking up by the river. Before the sun came up, not quite daylight, Uncle Johnny would build a fire and fire up a pan to fry some eggs for breakfast. He taught us how to fry them just right with a pinch of garlic salt on them. He loved cooking on the grill and we enjoyed eating whatever it was he cooked.

Being outdoors was my favorite place to be unless there was a storm rolling in. The only time I enjoyed a thunderstorm was when I was under the covers, safe in my room. I heard a lot of stories about people who died in thunderstorms, so I was really afraid of getting hit by lightning. Once the storm was over the next morning, I loved walking outside and stepping into a mud puddle in the driveway, watching the mud squish up through my toes. I loved that squishy feeling — it was the most satisfying feeling I could imagine.

My sisters and I loved playing with each other, and oftentimes we would play 'house' out in the hayloft, which made up the upper level of our barn. We would use the hay bales to create partitions and make them into 'rooms' for our' house'. One of us would be the 'dad' and another the 'mom' and of course the rest were the kids. We always had an abundance of cats and kittens on the farm, so we would dress the little kitties in doll clothes and pretend they were our babies. It was hard trying to get them to sit still while having our pretend church service. We got along well and those were fun, enjoyable, and carefree days.

I'll always and forever cherish the life I experienced with my big family on the farm. Growing up in a big family didn't give me much free time, but I enjoyed every free minute I did get. I'd go for a walk or ride horses or read my books. I passionately loved doing any of those activities. I greatly appreciate the sweet simplicity of life on the farm.

One of the schoolhouses I attended.

4.

At School

The day came when I was old enough to start school. We, as Amish, did not have kindergarten — we started our school years at first grade. Going to school with my brothers was a new and exciting experience.

Most of the time, an *Englisha* driver with a big van would pick up all the Amish kids and take them to their schools. Even though there were a lot of Amish kids that got on the bus and went to a public school, we never did. We attended a private Amish

Parochial School, which was taught by an *Englisha* who was certified to teach school, in the earlier years. But in my later years, our teachers were all Amish teachers.

I attended school in a one-room schoolhouse with all the students in all eight grades in one room. There were approximately twenty to twenty-six students per schoolroom. Since there is usually one school per church district, whenever we wanted to change churches, we had to move to the district where the new church was located, which also meant changing schools.

As a child, I changed schools three times. The last school I attended was taught by several different teachers throughout my years there. At times we had two teachers at the same time — one for the younger students and another for the older grades.

I had a hunger for learning new things, reading, writing, and spelling. I consumed everything I could, listening raptly to our teacher and reading every word in the lesson of the day. What

AT SCHOOL

I liked more than anything was recess time, where we would go outside and play games like 'Round Town', a form of softball, Kick the Can, and Peek Around the Corner.

I had lots of great friends at school, which made it fun. I didn't particularly appreciate it when I had to miss a day to help my Mom at home. I just wanted to hang out with my friends at recess, enjoying each other's company. We did a lot of light-hearted joking and laughing as we ate our lunches, planning our future together. We jokingly made plans to all live together instead of getting married.

Two of my best friends were a grade ahead of me. Their names were Clara and Rebecca. It was hard to keep from laughing during class — all it took was a mischievous grin from one of us. Clara was the sweetest, most calm, and caring friend anyone could ask for. I didn't know at the time that she would eventually be married to my cousin Noah, whom I grew up with. Clara was the kind of person everyone longs to have in their life, a lifelong, forever kind of friend.

On rainy days we'd play in the basement of the schoolhouse. One game we played down there was called 'Keep Away'. It consisted of two teams with one football. One day while playing this game, I got hit in the stomach with the ball and passed out. It knocked the air right out of me.

Needless to say, I was done for the day but I didn't have the luxury of going to the nurse's office because we didn't have any such thing in our little one-room schoolhouse. And there were no phones so we couldn't call Mom to come and pick me up. Even if we could have, it would've taken most of the day for her to catch the horse, hitch it up, and drive to the school. And so I toughed it out until the end of the day.

Getting hurt while playing a good game was just a rite of passage while growing up Amish. There's another game injury that I'll never forget, and I still have the scar to show for it. We were at my uncle's house and all of us kids were playing outside while the adults were inside. It was dark. During the game, I had to go to the restroom, so I went round to the back of the house. I found a spot in the shadows and made sure no one was around before I stooped down to pee by a bucket.

Little did I know, that bucket was full of broken sheets of glass. My butt caught on a jagged edge of glass and cut deep into the flesh of my butt cheek. I snuck into the house to show my Mom.

Mom said, "Oh my, we have to take you to the doctor! You need stitches!"

The cut was deep and bleeding heavily, but I was horrified at my Mom's suggestion. Instead of being worried about a tetanus infection or worse, I was embarrassed and terrified that anyone else might see my butt. If the doctor at the hospital was a man, that would be even worse. Amish girls do not show their butts to anyone. They are modest. I refused to go to the doctor that night and to this day, I have a long scar on my butt.

I was at the top of my class in school along with my first cousin, Noah. We always had our studies done before everyone else. He would do a lot of drawing in his free time while I read my beloved books. At one of the parent-teacher meetings, I overheard the teacher talking to my Mom about me as her student and suggested that I could skip a grade if I wanted to.

Now, for most children, that may have been a welcomed suggestion but, not for me. I knew I didn't want to skip a grade. I wanted to experience everything that I possibly could in each grade since we were only allowed an eighth-grade education.

I loved school and wanted to learn all that I possibly could. There were many times when those of us who were all caught up with our studies for the day were asked to help the teachers teach or to help a student who was struggling to catch up.

I had the experience of being a substitute teacher even while I was attending school. I especially enjoyed helping my friends who struggled or

AT SCHOOL

had learning disabilities. It was fulfilling to see the light bulb come on as they learned new things and improved their grades.

Holmes County, Ohio

5.
Trips to Ohio

One of the highlights of my life when I was growing up, was going to Holmes County, Ohio where my Grandpa Eicher and Step-Grandmother, Dena, lived with my Aunt Annamae and Uncle Norman, both of them younger than me. Grandma Dena was my grandpa's second wife. His first wife, Mary, passed away when my Dad was sixteen years old. I never knew her.

Our annual trip to Sugarcreek, Ohio was a four-hour drive. That seemed like an eternity for us since we didn't go on road trips very often. All of us piled into a van that was driven by an *Englisha* driver. We were a full vanload of people and it was always a relief to stop for bathroom breaks.

We all enjoyed the scenery while traveling the backroads of Holmes County. From the van windows, we watched a world go by that was different from our own. It was breathtakingly beautiful. I could never get tired of the beautiful rolling hills, freshly painted whiteboard fences where the cattle and horses grazed on green pastures, with well-manicured lawns in front of beautiful tree-lined driveways curving up to homes with porches filled with planters and greenery beside painted rocking chairs. I could envision myself sitting in them with a glass of iced tea and a good book to read. To me, that was living the dream.

We also loved the modern conveniences at Grandpa's house. There was running water in the sink and a toilet that flushed because his house had indoor plumbing. With soft cushioned chairs and pretty curtains, everything in Grandpa's house was beautiful. Even the food that Grandma prepared looked luscious and tasted just as wonderful.

My Grandpa Ben was very dear to me. His eyes twinkled above his wispy white beard when he looked at me and patted me on the head. Grandpa Ben was always happy to see me and my family, offering us delicious refreshments after our four-hour journey.

After serving us, he would brew himself a cup of sassafras tea. I can still remember the aroma that wafted up from his steaming cup. Sitting at the table and listening to him and my Dad visit and catch up on all the goings-on in the family gave me a sense of comfort and security. I love the family values that were instilled in us at that young age. It's a priceless trait that no amount of money could ever buy.

After enjoying our refreshments, I joined my siblings outside where we took turns riding bicycles up and down the driveway. Oh my goodness!

This was such a fun treat for us since the Amish church we belonged to back in Indiana did not allow bicycles. We took turns riding back and forth, up and down the steep hill. Now I realize now how dangerous it was since grandpa's house was situated on a bustling highway, but we didn't think of that then. We were inexperienced on those bikes, and it was very dangerous to come speeding down the hill, right toward the highway, and stopping right before we got to the end of the long driveway.

One of my brothers learned his lesson the hard way when he couldn't stop in time. He and the bike landed sideways on the highway and the oncoming car swerved so as not to run over my brother. We were all frightened and shaking like leaves. Thankfully, he wasn't injured. We were definitely more careful after that near accident.

....

Sometimes when we'd spend the weekend

TRIPS TO OHIO

GRANDPA'S HOUSE

This is the place where my siblings and I created many wonderful memories.

in Ohio, we'd go to the Swiss festival. Small bands and artists set up stages amongst the crowd to play music and yodel. People came from miles around to visit the craft booths, dance to the music, and eat Swiss Food. Through the Swiss festivals, I was introduced to new and exciting things. What fun that was! My Dad loved going to the cheese factory. He'd take us inside, where we watched the cheese being made right before our eyes! I watched in awe as the enormous stainless steel containers with the large metal beaters went round and round, stirring the hundreds of gallons of thick milk as they made it into cheese. And then there was the Trail Bologna! Dad loved these two items together: Baby Swiss cheese and Trail Bologna. He always bought lots of it to take home with us.

That was one thing my Dad was always passionate about — food, lots of food. And he loved to share his love of food with others. It never failed; when visitors stopped by, Dad would always offer them a bite to eat or something to drink. Both of my parents were very generous, always doing something for us kids and others.

Not only did my Dad love food, but he was also passionate about music. He had many friends, some who were not Amish, and played musical instruments. We would often have a big crowd of people come to our house for a hog roast. I'll never forget those fun times. There was lots of food, fun, and music. The people would come with horses in the horse trailers and guitars and, of course, their coolers full of cold drinks. The women would bring lots and lots of food to the tables that had been set up outside. There were people everywhere, kids and grown-ups mingling collectively, and everyone seemed to enjoy themselves.

Us kids would ride horses while the men played their guitars and sang. Riding horses was a passion of mine. My favorite one to ride was brown and white, and her name was Dolly. Riding her put me in another world. I loved riding Dolly through the open fields, full stretch gallop. I had no fear; I just remember the feel of the wind in my face as I held the reins and let her run as fast as she could go. It was pure pleasure.

My twin brothers entertained everyone with their cute little ponies, who also looked like twins. They were very competitive and loved racing each other. They did the barrel racing as well as harness racing on the sulkey carts. It was definitely entertaining, to say the least.

The 'Corner Table' at my wedding.

6.

My Teenage Years

Summertime was always fun, especially when my Dad would take the whole family to fun places. Dad grabbed every opportunity to make good memories in life, and every summer he'd take us to the lakes or somewhere fun. He did some construction work for a farmer who owned a big stock truck with an open back end. It could hold as many as 30 people. We, along with several of Dad's employees and their families, would pile into the back of the truck and drive off to the lakes where we stayed all day long, swimming, riding speed boats, and having picnics. I'll never forget those hot summer days at the beach, walking in the sand with my bare feet, feeling the misty water as it hit my face, and relishing in the breeze from the lake. Oh, the joys of summertime at the beach. Dad knew how to make life fun and we all enjoyed these fun outings.

It was always a pleasure to go to work with Dad. He often needed all the help he could get when he was doing work for chicken farmers who needed as many hands as they could find to help carry the chickens and load them into crates on big semi-trucks.

Whenever we helped Dad, we always knew that we would get to eat in a real, sit-down restaurant where we could order whatever food we wanted, which usually included one of my favorites — french fries. This was always the highlight of the day and made work seem like fun.

My Dad did a lot of construction and remodeling work and build new pole barns. It was simple work that we could help with, so he would take some of us kids along with him to work from a young age. It wasn't long until my brothers and I would ask to help run the screw guns as he hung the sheets of metal for siding. We learned many things like this at a very young age.

By the time I was a teenager, we had grown into a large family, which shifted responsibilities, and we older kids started to get jobs of our own.

The first babysitting job I had at the age of fourteen required me to stay with *'English people'* for a week at a time. This was new to me. I had never been away from home for more than a night or two at a time, so a whole week away from my family felt almost unbearable. Crying myself to sleep at night, I laid in bed and counted the days when I could go home again.

It was easier to cope with my feelings of loneliness in the daytime because I kept myself busy with the household chores and I also had television to watch. Watching TV was new for me since we didn't have electricity or any modern conveniences at home. I would soon find myself getting hooked on soap operas like *The Guiding Light* or *Days of Our Lives*. It didn't take long for me to get all wrapped up in TV drama.

On the weekends, Dad's employees and '*English friends*' came over to sit around and drink with Dad. One of them asked me how old I was while I was sitting on the porch swing, pushing myself back and forth with my tan bare feet.

I tucked a wisp of my dark-colored hair under my Amish cap as I replied that I was fourteen years old.

He winked at me and said, "I wish I was fifteen with a really good horse and buggy."

Another weekend, another one of Dad's friends asked me how old I was.

"Fourteen," I said again, to which he replied that he wished I was 16.

Then I asked him, "Well, how old are you?"

He sighed a long sigh and said, "Forty-one."

He took another sip of his beer. Another man commented, "She'd make a nice filly."

I wasn't exactly sure why the men asked me questions or make the comments they did, but it made me feel a mixture of feelings.

My Dad enjoyed listening to us girls sing, yodel, and play the harmonica. When family or his friends would come over, he'd ask us to sign for them. My sister Christina would usually lead, and I would harmonize with her. Our sister Mary was good at yodeling in harmony with us, and we all played the harmonica on occasion.

There were times when we didn't feel like singing to entertain the guests, so Dad would promise us gifts for doing it and sure enough, he'd come home from work with nice little gifts for us.

Both of my parents came from large families, so I had an abundance of aunts and uncles. I adored my aunts. It was always a treat for me to spend time with Aunt Barbara, my Mom's sister. She and her husband always made me feel welcome and wanted. They had tried to have children but it just wasn't happening, so I was willing to fill in as a daughter.

I was extra close to Aunt Barbara. She was always happy — always smiling or laughing. I had such a fun time at their house, where we would get into their swimming pool after a hot day in the field. I'll never forget the blistering sunburn on my back on one of those occasions when I stayed in the pool too long. That was very painful. It hurt so bad I could hardly sleep that night.

Aunt Barbara adored her husband. She worked in the barn and fields alongside him. They had a big barn full of farm animals: horses, sheep, cows, pigs, and chickens. She would always allow me to gather the eggs from the hen house. I can still hear the squawking of the chickens as we shooed them out of their nests to gather their eggs. They didn't seem to appreciate us taking their eggs from them, and then there was always a bandy rooster or two in the bunch. They sometimes made me nervous as they would fight each other and chase us out of the chicken coop.

The best advantage of spending time at Aunt Barbara's house was that I had her and my uncle's undivided attention since they didn't have children of their own. It's something I wasn't used to since I had so many siblings. They took an interest in me and my life and not only talked to me but listened to what I had to say. It made me feel loved and heard, and cared for.

I often wondered what it would have been like to be an only child, and staying with my aunt and uncle kind of gave me an idea of what it would look like. I concluded that it has its advantages and disadvantages. I was always delighted to go back home to my siblings, where there was never a dull moment.

As Amish young people, we were required to give our paychecks to our parents until we reached the accountability age of twenty-one or until we would get married, whichever came first. We never knew any different, and so when I turned sixteen, my parents got me a real job working in the kitchen at the local bar in town.

Even though I enjoyed cooking, I was not too fond of this job. Every time I would take the clean glasses out front into the bar area, there were always drunk men staring at me or trying to flirt with me, which caused me to feel dirty. Tommie was one of the owners of the bar. She was a Spanish-speaking woman. She would come back to the kitchen where I was busy cooking and doing dishes, she'd hand me some quarters and in her broken English, she'd say, "Irene, go play the jukebox!" You know all the good songs. Of course, I didn't mind since I loved music.

There were times I couldn't wait to get out of there. They never allowed me to leave one minute early, not even when Mark, my boyfriend, would come to pick me up. He stood outside and waited for me. I vowed I'd never ask a child of my own to work at a bar.

THE TEENAGE YEARS

....

My sisters and I had many friends. Our favorite social outings were going to church or weddings. I loved dressing up when we would go to such events. My way of 'dressing up' consisted of wearing a black bonnet and a specific pattern of dress which I sewed myself, I am proud to say.

We had several different colors of dresses we were allowed to wear. My favorite dress was yellow, and I wore it with a white starched cape and apron. We secured our aprons and dresses with straight pins. I'll forever remember the stings as the pins pierced my skin. Whoever came up with that idea obviously never held their clothes in place with straight pins.

At the age of sixteen, Amish young people start 'rumspringa' or as we called it, 'going to the crowd' days. This is a period of time where Amish young people explore their independence before officially joining the Amish church.

I eagerly anticipated joining my older brothers, who had been going to the crowd for a year already and seemed to be having so much fun. Since I was the oldest girl, I would be the first one out of my sisters to start rumspringa.

I listened with rapt attention to my brothers as they discussed the events that happened on Sunday night. They talked about who took beautiful Sarah home for a date or about plain Sam who wanted pretty Katie but she turned him down for the tall, handsome Jake. It all sounded romantic and exciting. They would talk about Johnny's fast horse or David's shiny new buggy with the hidden speakers under the seat, which was completely forbidden. David liked to live life on the wild side.

Once I started rumspringa, I too enjoyed sharing all the details of the happenings of the crowds with my younger sisters. They were not yet old enough to go, so when Monday morning came, I would relate stories to them as we did the dishes or laundry or whatever task we were assigned. They listened with anticipation as I told them about being asked out by whomever it was the night before or as I talked about the fun we had playing 'Huddleshtrow. They could hardly wait until they could join me in the fun.

Having any musical instruments was against the rules of the church, except for the harmonica. Lots of our young people were quite accomplished harmonica players, some extremely talented. This was one of the joys of a Sunday night crowd — listening to the harmonica players along with the singing and yodeling.

There was hardly anything more fun on a summer night, especially when the crowd was taking place out in a barn where the floor had been cleared for dancing or the 'Huddleshtrow' as it was called in our language. We'd partner up and dance long into the night. Many times I'd wake up on a Monday morning with sore, aching arms, but I didn't mind. The fun we had was worth any pain I endured.

I met Mark at an Amish house, where the

crowd was on a Sunday evening. He was a handsome young Amish man with strong arms, big hands, broad shoulders, and a head full of light brown hair. When he saw me for the first time, he knew that I would be his wife. But I didn't know that. He ditched his girlfriend to take me home. His girlfriend was sobbing as if her heart would break, and I just wanted him to take her back. He still had to get my brothers to convince me to date him.

I was still a couple of months shy of turning sixteen the first time Mark asked me to date him. He took me out behind the chicken coup and asked me to go out with him sometime. I said no. He was from a different church district, and I was too young to be in a committed relationship. The second time he asked me out, I said yes. I didn't want to be an old maid and Mark wanted me, so we started dating.

On our first date, he took me home on a Sunday evening and we went up to my room, where we made out in my bed for a while. He forgot his

THE TEENAGE YEARS

GRANDMA ANNIE'S HOUSE

This is one of the first places Mark took me when we started dating. He loved his grandmother. Grandma Annie was the sweetest lady I've ever known. She LOVED everyone.

hat and had to come to get it in the middle of the week. Maybe he did that on purpose so he could see me again. Mark was completely smitten with me and he couldn't stay away.

After that, we never went more than a few days without seeing each other. I got pregnant a few months later, at just sixteen years old, and we got married a month after my seventeenth birthday, making me a child bride. I would spend the rest of my teenage years being a wife and mother.

....

In our Amish culture, the young people would be expected to start 'following church' at the age of sixteen in order to become members. 'Following church' meant to take instruction classes. Every other week, we would follow the Bishop and his ministers to a separate room where they read the Articles of Faith. There are eighteen of them. Since church was held bi-weekly and they taught one article each time, it would take at least thirty-six weeks to prepare for baptism. Once the classes were completed, the young people would be baptized into the Amish church, becoming a member for life.

If, for some reason, a young person decided that they weren't ready to join the church at that age, they were considered rebellious. An Amish young couple could not get married until they were members. That is also when the guys were required to start growing their beards. For the most part, the majority of the young folks would comply with the church rules without rebelling or questioning the reasons why.

'Following church' was different for me because I got pregnant at sixteen, before I could join the church with the rest of my peers. The church made an exception and rushed me through the process. Since I had to be baptized before Mark and I could get married, I was baptized on my wedding day.

We had always been discouraged from asking too many questions about our faith. I was always told, "That's just the way we've been taught, or who are we to question what our forefathers taught us?" And so I was content to follow the traditions of our forefathers for the time being. But the time would come when I would search for truth and would be willing to forsake all to follow Jesus and learn the true meaning of the word of God. The *best* was yet to come.

Meet The Author

Eirene, a young Amish girl, grew up on a farm in a rural, Old Order Amish community in Geneva IN. Being the oldest girl in a family of sixteen children, she worked very hard. She also played hard and loved every minute. She never thought she would ever leave her beloved community where she felt content serving her family. In fact, she never wanted to leave the safe haven of her Amish community until she began her search for Truth.

Also by Eirene Eicher

LEAVING MY AMISH WORLD

LIFE AFTER LEAVING MY AMISH WORLD

Connect with Eirene

WWW.EIRENEEICHER.COM

EICHERIRENE7@GMAIL.COM

Printed in Great Britain
by Amazon